Mexi Cookbook

The Complete Mexican Cookbook. Tasty Recipes for Real Home Cooking. Discover Mexican Food Culture and Enjoy the Authentic Flavors. Traditional and Modern Recipes for all Tastes.

By
Mark Stone

Legal Disclaimer

The information contained in this book and its contents is not designed to replace any form of medical or professional advice; and is not meant to replace the need for independent medical, financial, legal, or other professional advice or services that may be required. The content and information in this book have been provided for educational and entertainment purposes only.

The content and information contained in this book have been compiled from sources deemed reliable, and they are accurate to the best of the Author's knowledge, information, and belief. However, the Author cannot guarantee its accuracy and validity and therefore cannot be held liable for any errors and/or omissions. Further, changes are periodically made to this book as needed. Where appropriate and/or necessary, you must consult a professional (including but not limited to your doctor, attorney, financial advisor, or other such professional) before using any of the suggested remedies, techniques, and/or information in this book.

Upon using this book's contents and information, you agree to hold harmless the Author from any damages, costs, and expenses, including any legal fees potentially resulting from the application of any of the information in this

Table of Contents

Introduction

Whenever we talk of Mexican cuisine, it is tacos, quesadillas, enchiladas, burritos that come to our mind. The cuisine dates back to a whopping 9000 years ago and though things have changed drastically ever since the Mexican cuisine continues to remain extremely popular among people.

In this book, we are going to share some of the finest Mexican recipes which will help you relish the perfect taste of the meals and perfectly enjoy the cuisine.

When you go through this book, you will be able to capture some of the best details about the finest and the most authentic Mexican recipes. So, even if you have a BBQ party or people coming to your house, you would have the best set of recipes to guide you in the right manner. We are sure that this will impress you and we want you to stick to the recipes as much as you can. Doing this will help you infuse your dish with the perfect flavor and thereby relish the perfect taste of the authentic Mexican meals.

Remember, when it comes to Mexican dishes, it is as much about the sauce as it is about the dish. So, be very mindful of what you are adding because the spices surely make for a very important part of this aspect.

So, if you seem to have a thing for cooking and you would like to have the best taste of Mexican food on your mouth, make the most of this cookbook. We believe that every recipe here is one of the very best and has been picked after careful consideration. The massive variety means that you will always have something or the other to look forward to.

So, are you all set to open your kitchen to a world of endless delicious dishes and some of the most lip-smacking recipes of all time? Do not be counting your calories right away as we will make sure to mix and match the recipes and pitch in with a lot of healthy choices too. So, if you happen to be a fitness freak, you still have every reason to smile and peruse through this book.

So, are you all set to get your hands on some of the finest Mexican recipes which will stir perfectness in your kitchen?

Chapter 1: Mexican Culture

Mexican culture is rich and boasts of a massive variety. Not just food, even when we talk of other things, Mexican ideology is all about spice, flavor, and enjoying life the way it comes.

The best thing about the Mexican culture is that you can find influences of several different cultures in it. It is this amalgamation and confluence of too many different geographical aspects which perhaps gives it one of the most unique styles.

The History

Back in the 1500s, when the Europeans had come to Mexico, the natives of the country primarily composed of Aztecs and Maya had their staple diet. This was mainly tomatoes, pepper, beans, herbs and more. It is interesting to add that the drink fit for royals was chocolate which happens to be native to Mexico.

The Mexican culture has the maximum Spanish dominance to it as the Spanish infused their style to Mexican history, culture, and food. They are credited with introducing cattle, livestock, pigs, chickens and more to the typical Mexican cuisine. Spain continued to rule over Mexico for massive three centuries and thus it is no surprise that even today, in large parts of Mexico, you can find the Spanish touch; no matter whether we talk of people, their cuisine and even their culture.

The Mexican Food

Mexicans love to gorge on great food. Food is very popular in Mexico and such is their amazingly delicious meal that Mexican food enjoys widespread popularity all over the world. Even if you head to the core parts of America, tacos and quesadillas are going to be found at every nook and corner of the city.

But, when we talk of the core Mexican food, it comes down to corn. For more than thousands of years, corn has been regarded as the staple and the basic Mexican diet. This is why most of the recipes we will be talking of in this book are likely to feature corn. Tortilla beans, nachos are the munchies most kids grow upon.

When we are talking about Mexican cuisine, there is no way we can miss out on the spices and the sauces. This cuisine is hailed for gifting the world some of the finest variety of sauces. Whenever you savor an amazing dip with a dish, you can be pretty sure that it is very likely to be Mexican favor. It is the use of right spices and herbs which is known to infuse the best of flavor in these dishes. So, Mexican cuisine is a lot about picking the right ingredients and infusing it with the perfect flavor and aroma.

Jalapeno, chipotle, Serrano, and pepper are widely used in most Mexican style of cooking and you are going to find them in abundance when we discuss the best of recipes.

So, when we talk of Mexican cuisine, you are bound to see the strong influence of both native indigenous Indian taste and the Spanish influence as well. There are a few dishes which enjoy more popularity as compared to others and they are consumed at large by young and old people alike.

The good thing about Mexican cuisine has to be the whopping variety which you are bound to find. Most Mexicans are massive lovers of food and this infers that they are always ready to host a lavish meal and make some of the best kinds of preparations to indulge in a great cooking show.

The Culture Of Street Food

When in Mexico, there is no way you will be able to miss out on the rich culture of street food. Once again, be prepared to see endless stalls that make the best of pambazos, alambres, tacos, quesadillas, and more. There is no doubt that when you hover around the street side food corners, you are sure to witness a massive American influence too as a lot of fast food seems to be inspired by the American lifestyle, culture, and eating habits. This had happened since the late 20th century as the hot dog seems to have gained quite a lot of popularity in large parts of Mexico. But, even when you are gorging on a hot dog, the exact style and taste will be hard to miss as they may go really easy on the peppers and spices.

Not just food, you can find a plethora of different drinks at the food stalls too. All in all, when in Mexico, there is no way you will miss out on the true pleasure of eating some of the best possible food and treating your food buds to the finest possible cuisine.

Of course, different parts of Mexico will show different kinds of culture and the differences can be traced in the eating pattern as well. So, it is upon you to explore the length and breadth of Mexico and keep an eye out for the common food types in different areas.

Doing this will help you choose the perfect places and the right cuisines and dishes which are famous in that area. We believe that of all the different pleasures and luxuries in life, it is food which most people tend to cherish the most. The sheer pleasure when you are able to spot the kind of food which makes your food buds break into a happy dance is inexplicable.

Some countries like Mexico, America, Italy, India are known to be the true home that boasts of the best of food and this is why when you are traveling in Mexico, you will be all set to have a great deal of fun.

So, now that we have set the base regarding why Mexican food is such a rage, we are going to share some of the most amazing recipes. We will make sure to segment the recipes into several sections so that you can pursue the ones you wish to and try your hand at cooking some of the best possible choices.

Be all set to pay heed to every minute detail because like we have mentioned Mexican food is all about getting the ingredients right and infusing it with the perfect mix.

Chapter 2: Typical Mexican Dishes

First of all, let us start the recipe list with some of the typical Mexican dishes which enjoy a great amount of popularity. These are the perfect recipes which you should try first when you are looking for authentic Mexican dishes to savor.

Churro Chips

These are surely the go-to choice for most Mexicans. No matter whether you are glued to your seats watching sports or even movies, this is the munchies you are likely to devour.

Ingredients

- 6 mid flour tortillas
- 1 cup of granulated sugar
- 4 tbsp of melted butter
- 1 ½ tbsp of cinnamon

Instructions

- Preheat your oven to 425 degrees.
- Now take the tortilla and cut them into 8 different triangles
- Toss these cut tortillas in butter and when doing so make sure that both the sides get coated evenly
- Now take a fresh bowl and mix cinnamon and sugar in it
- Take some tortillas and toss them in the mix
- Repeat this process in batches
- Now take a large baking sheet and place the tossed tortillas on it
- Bake them for 8 to10 minutes till they turn crisp
- Let it cool for 5 minutes
- Serve

Mexican Taco Pizza

When it comes to typical Mexican dishes, there is no way we cannot mention pizza. To be honest, this is a very loose adaptation of the word pizza; still, let us share the details of this quick recipe.

Ingredients

- ½ lb of ground beef
- 6 medium flour tortillas
- ¼ cup of black olives; sliced
- 2 thinly sliced green onions
- ½ cup of cherry tomatoes; quartered
- 1 ½ cup of refried beans
- 1 ½ cup of shredded cheese
- 2 tbsp of taco seasoning
- Kosher salt
- Black pepper
- Sour cream
- Hot sauce

Instructions

- Preheat the oven to 375 degrees
- Take a medium-sized baking sheet and line it with parchment paper
- Now take a large skillet and heat it on medium flame
- Add ground beef to it while making sure that the meat gets broken
- Cook it for nearly 5 minutes until the beef doesn't look pink anymore
- Drain away the excess fat
- Return it to the flame and sprinkle taco seasoning on it and then season it with salt and pepper
- Cook it for one more minute before removing it from the flame
- Now take a baking sheet and keep 3 tortillas on it
- Spread nearly ¼ cup of refried beans over the tortillas
- Divide the beef evenly between the tortillas and then sprinkle ¼ cup of cheese over each of them
- Top it now with the leftover tortillas
- Spread bean and cheese by putting a layer again
- Bake it for 10 to 12 minutes until the beans get warm
- Garnish with tomatoes, onions, olives, sour cream
- Serve along with a hot sauce

Cheesy Chicken Enchiladas

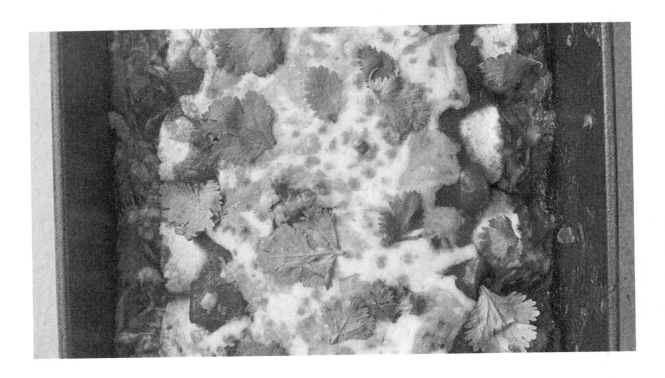

Enchiladas is hailed to be one of the most typical, common, and popular Mexican recipes. It is the popular pick for most Mexicans and the taste is so good that you are going to be hooked as well.

Ingredients

- 3 cup of chicken; cooked and shredded
- 12 corn tortillas
- 8 oz can have crushed tomatoes
- 1 chopped red bell pepper
- ½ chopped onion
- 2 cup of divided shredded cheddar cheese
- 2 cup of shredded and divided Monterey jack
- 1 tsp of cumin
- 2 clove of minced garlic
- 1 tbsp of extra virgin olive oil
- 10 oz can of red enchilada sauce
- ¼ cup of cilantro; freshly chopped
- Kosher salt

Instructions

- Preheat the oven to 350 degrees
- Take a large skillet (oven proof) and place it on medium flame
- Heat oil in it and then add onion and pepper to it until the onion turns translucent
- Now add cumin and garlic and let it cook for a minute
- Add enchilada sauce to it and also add crushed tomatoes and cook it till it warms well
- Set aside ½ cup of this sauce to be used as topping later
- Now take a mid-sized bowl and add chicken along with cheddar, 1 cup of Monterey jack and cilantro
- Add 1 cup of the sauce mixture made before and toss well to mix
- Season it with salt
- Now take a small scoop of the chicken mixture and place it at the center of the tortillas
- Roll it up and then place the seam side down in the skillet containing the sauce
- Repeat the process with the rest of the tortillas
- Take the reserved 1/ 2 cup of sauce and sprinkle on top of the tortillas and add cheese
- Bake it for 10 minutes
- Garnish with the right amount of cilantro and serve

Tacos Al Pastor

Now, this isn't the easiest of tacos to make, but trust us when we say, the taste is so good that you will find yourself cooking it several times a week.

Ingredients

For the achiote paste

- 5 allspice berries
- 1/4 cup of annatto seeds
- 1 tbsp of cumin seeds
- 1 tbsp of coriander seeds
- 1 tsp of mustard seeds
- 2 tbsp of apple cider vinegar
- 1/3 cup of orange juice
- 1/4 cup of extra-virgin olive oil
- 4 cloves of garlic
- 1 tsp of kosher salt
- 2 tsp of dried oregano
- 1 tsp of black peppercorns

For the pork

- 2 lb boneless pork shoulder, sliced 1/2" thick
- 3 dried de-seeded chiles de Arbol
- 3 dried de-seeded guajillo chilis
- 3 cloves of garlic
- 1/4 cup of achiote paste
- 1 tbsp extra-virgin olive oil
- 1/3 cup of pineapple juice
- 2 tbsp of apple cider vinegar

- 1 tsp of ground cinnamon
- 2 tbsp of packed brown sugar
- 2 tsp of kosher salt
- 1/2 tsp of freshly ground black pepper

For serving

- 1 cored pineapple; cut into even-sized rings
- 12 corn tortillas
- 1 red onion; cut into even-sized rings
- Cilantro; freshly chopped
- Lime wedges

Instructions

Making the Achiote paste

- Take a small skillet and place it on the medium flame.
- Add coriander along with cumin, annatto seeds, mustard seeds, oregano, allspice berries, and peppercorns and toast it for a minute
- Take a blender and add the toasted seeds along with vinegar, orange juice, garlic, and salt
- Blend it till you get a smooth paste

Making the tacos

- Take a small-sized skillet and place it on medium flame
- Heat oil in it
- Now add chilies and toast it slightly for a minute
- Take a blender and add the toasted chilis along with achiote paste, garlic, pineapple juice, salt, pepper, vinegar, cinnamon, and brown sugar
- Blend till you get a smooth mix
- Now take a large bowl and add pork to it. Pour marinade over it and cover it well. Refrigerate it overnight
- Preheat the grill by keeping it on medium-high flame. Brush it with oil
- Grill the pork till it has cooked well. It should be done approximately 5 minutes per side
- Now leave it on the cutting board for 5 minutes and then cut them evenly into 1" pieces

- Add onions and then place it on the grill and cook it till it has softened
- Add the tortilla to the grill and cook it a minute per side
- On these tortillas add pork, onions, pineapple, and cilantro
- Serve with lime wedges

Chicken Pozole

When we talk of typical Mexican dishes, there is no way we can miss out on the top comfort food. This is one such soup that is known to be loved by all Mexicans and the taste is so yum that you will find yourself making it more often than you thought you would.

Ingredients

- 3 chicken breasts; boneless, skinless
- 4 cup of chicken broth; low-sodium
- 2 cup (15-oz.) can of drained hominy
- 1 chopped white onion
- 2 cloves of minced garlic
- 1 tbsp of cumin
- 2 tsp of chili powder
- 1 tbsp of oregano
- 2 tsp of kosher salt
- Freshly ground black pepper
- 2 chopped poblano peppers
- Thinly sliced radishes, for garnish
- Fresh cilantro, for garnish
- Sliced green cabbage, for garnish

Instructions

- Take a slow cooker and add all ingredients to it except hominy and the ones for garnishing
- Now let it cook on low for 6 to 8 hours
- Take the chicken out of the cooker and then shred it slowly with the help of a fork
- Return it to the cooker and add hominy and cook further for half an hour
- Serve the soup into bowls and garnish with radish, cilantro, and cabbage

Burrito Egg Rolls

Egg rolls and burritos are a deadly mix and no one can resist this combination. They are the best choice hands down when you have a party coming and the guests are sure to go ga-ga over your excellent recipe!

Ingredients

- ½ lb of ground beef
- 12 egg roll wrappers
- ½ cup of frozen corn
- ½ cup of rinsed and drained black beans
- 1 seeded and diced small-sized tomato
- 2 cup of cheddar cheese; shredded
- 1 tsp of extra virgin olive oil
- Vegetable oil for frying
- Guacamole oil for serving
- 1 tsp of taco seasoning
- Kosher salt
- Ground black pepper
- ½ cup of green pepper hot sauce

Instructions

- Take a small-sized skillet and heat olive oil in it over medium to high flame
- Now add ground beef to it and sprinkle taco seasoning
- Season it with the right amount of salt and pepper
- Cook the meat for 5 minutes approx making sure to break it
- Drain away the excess fat and return the beef to the skillet once again
- Now add corn and black beans and cook it for a couple of minutes
- Move it to a medium-sized bowl and allow it to cool
- Now add the green pepper sauce and cheddar to the mixture comprising of ground beef and fold it in tomato
- Take the egg roll wrapper and set it in a diamond shape and spoon ¼ cup of the burrito mixture right in the very center
- Fold the bottom half and the sides and roll it gently making sure to seal the ends with the help of water drops
- Repeat this with the rest of the filling and wrapper
- Take a large skillet and heat vegetable oil over medium flame
- Now add egg rolls and fry it till they turn golden. Do this process in batches
- Drain them on a plate lined with a clean paper towel and allow them to cool
- Serve warm with guacamole

Chapter 3: Mexican Appetizer Recipes

There is something amazingly great about appetizers as it sets the tone for the rest of the meals and makes you gorge on them and enjoy it to the fullest. Here, we are going to share the recipes for some of the finest Mexican appetizers which will surely leave you asking for more.

Nachos Loaded Potato Skin

This perfect appetizer will have you licking your fingers and your guests are going to munch on it heavily as well.

Ingredients

- 6 strips of bacon
- 12 baby potatoes
- ½ cup of chopped scallions
- 1 cup of refried beans
- 6 tbsp of divided olive oil
- 1 cup of chipotle salsa
- 1 ½ cup of shredded cheddar cheese
- 1 tsp of garlic powder
- 1 tsp of red pepper flakes
- 1 cup of chipotle guacamole
- Sour cream

Instructions

- Preheat the oven to 400 degrees
- Now take the whole potatoes and place them on a baking sheet. Drizzle them with 1 tbsp of olive oil
- Bake for nearly half an hour till they turn tender
- When the potatoes are still being baked, cook 6 pieces of bacon till they turn crisp and then set them aside
- When it has cooled down, chop the bacon
- Now take the potatoes and remove them from the oven and let them cool
- Cut them in half and scoop out most of the insides while making sure that ¼ inch of it is left
- Now heat the oven to 450 degrees F
- Take the cut potatoes and place them back on the baking sheet, make sure that the cut side faces upwards
- Drizzle the top with the olive oil and sprinkle a little garlic powder along with red pepper flakes and then keep them back in the oven for 5 minutes
- Flip them and bake for 5 more minutes
- Now take the potatoes and arrange them on the baking sheet while making sure that the cut side faces upwards
- Spoon an equal amount of refried beans in each of the potatoes and follow it with bacon and shredded cheese.

- Place the skins back in the oven for 3 minutes till the cheese melts properly
- Now take them out and top them with salsa, guacamole, and sour cream along with scallions
- Serve

Easy Taco Sliders

You are never going to get bored with tacos, are you? When it comes to the Mexican cookbook, the amount of variation you will see with tacos is simply going to blow your mind away!

Ingredients

- 12 connected dinner rolls
- 1 lb of taco meat
- ½ cup of the diced bell pepper; yellow
- 1 cup of sour cream
- ½ cup of grape tomatoes; sliced
- ½ cup of melted stick butter
- ¼ cup of sliced hot jalapeno poppers
- 2 cup of divided taco cheese; shredded
- 1 tsp of garlic powder
- 1 tsp of onion powder
- ½ tsp of crushed red pepper

Instructions

- Preheat the oven to 350 degrees
- Take a pan and have cooking spray over it
- Slice the rolls like we do to a burger bun and keep the bottom half in the pan while keeping the top half aside
- Spread sour cream all over the bottom of the roll and make sure to evenly spread out the taco meat all over the sour cream
- Now sprinkle 1 cup of cheese over the taco meat
- Add peppers and tomatoes on the cheese
- Place the roll tops back on the bun and mix the melted butter along with garlic powder, onion powder, and red pepper
- Cover with aluminum foil and let it sit for some time
- Bake for 10 minutes
- Serve hot

Skilled Steak Fajita Nachos

This is likely to be a heavy appetizer and could also double up as a main course depending on the kind of appetite you have. Regardless of which course you use it for, there is no denying the perfect taste that you are sure to get along with it.

Ingredients

- 1 large bag of tortilla chips
- 1 lb. of flank steak
- 1 chopped red pepper
- 2 chopped onions
- ¼ cup fresh chopped cilantro
- 1 chopped green pepper
- 1 packet of 1-ounce Old El Paso Taco Seasoning
- 1 can of 4.5-ounce Old El Paso green chilies
- 1 cup of pico de gallo
- 8 ounces of Mexican blend cheese
- 4 tbsp of fresh lime juice
- 1/3 cup of olive oil
- 1 tbsp of minced garlic
- Guacamole sour cream, more cilantro, and pico de gallo for garnish

Instructions

- Take a blender and add taco seasoning, olive oil, green chiles, garlic, lime juice, and cilantro.
- Blend it well until it has mixed thoroughly and there is a smooth consistency.
- Now place the flank steak in a large zip lock bag and add in the marinade. Make sure to keep some for the vegetables
- Place it in the fridge overnight
- Take out the steak and cook it on a skillet for 5 mixtures approximately. Make sure to do it on each side
- Remove it from the skillet and cut it into small bite-sized pieces which you need to keep aside
- Take the skillet again and add in green pepper, red pepper, and onion to it.
- Pour the leftover marinade in it and sauté on medium to high flame for 3 to 5 minutes till you find that the onions have turned a little translucent
- Place it on a plate and keep it aside
- Now to this same skillet itself, add the tortilla chips. Top those with half the cheese and the pepper onion mixture prepared above.
- Add steak to it and then add the leftover cheese.
- Top it further with cilantro and pico de gallo
- Now bake the nachos in the oven on high for 5 minutes and check if the cheese has melted

- Serve after topping with cilantro, guacamole, and sour cream

Avocado Black Bean Quesadillas

This is one of the most delicious combinations we could think of and we are sure that everyone will absolutely love to munch it! With a total cooking time of fewer than 20 minutes, this could be your go-to appetizer for a lot of occasions.

Ingredients

- 4 mid-sized soft flour tortillas
- 2 peeled, halved, sliced, seeded avocados
- ½ sliced bell pepper
- ½ cup of drained black beans
- ½ sliced onion
- 1 lime; cut into half
- 1 tbsp of taco seasoning
- 1 tbsp of olive oil
- 1 cup of mozzarella cheese
- ¼ cup of cilantro; minced

Instructions

- Take a medium pan and place it on mid-high flame and sauté bell pepper and onion in it for a couple of minutes till they turn tender
- Now add black beans along with taco seasoning
- Cook for one minute
- Take this whole thing into another bowl and let it set aside
- Now clean the pan and bring it back to the flame. Drizzle it with a little cooking spray
- Take a small bowl and add avocados and mash them with a fork
- Mix the cilantro along with the juice of ½ lime and season it with salt and pepper
- Spread a quarter of the avocados that have been mashed on the half of a tortilla
- Top it with bean mixture and ¼ cup of cheese
- Fold the tortilla and close it over the veggies
- Repeat this till you do it with all the tortillas
- Cook it on medium to high flame for a couple of minutes per side
- Serve with your favorite dip

South-Western Egg Rolls

If you are looking for a healthy snack that is filled with loads of veggies to give your health the right push; this is surely the perfect appetizer to crush on.

Ingredients

- 1 package of egg roll wrappers; 21 count pack
- 1 ½ cups of chicken breast; cooked and diced
- ½ cup of frozen spinach thawed and excess water squeezed out
- ¼ cup of green onions; sliced
- 1 cup of red bell pepper; finely diced
- 1 cup of black beans
- 1 cup of corn kernels
- 2 cups of shredded Monterey Jack cheese
- ½ tsp of ground cumin
- 2 tsp of chili powder
- ¼ cup of jalapeno peppers; seeded and minced
- 1 tsp of salt
- ¼ tsp of black pepper

For the avocado ranch sauce

- ½ cup of avocado
- 1 cup of ranch dressing
- 1/3 cup of cilantro leaves
- Salt and pepper as per taste

Instructions

- Take a bowl and mix the corn along with jalapeño pepper, red pepper, spinach, green onion, beans, chicken, cumin, cheese, chili powder, salt, and pepper
- Now take one egg roll wrapper and keep it on the cutting board
- Add 2 heaping tbsp on the wrapper and roll it as per the instructions mentioned on the package. Seal it tight with the use of little water
- Repeat this process with the leftover egg roll wrappers
- Now place these rolls on a pan which has been lined with parchment sheet
- Cover it and set it free for a couple of hours
- Take a large skillet and heat it over medium flame
- Pour the oil on the pan and then heat it to 350 degrees F
- Place nearly 4 to 5 egg rolls in the pan and then cook it approx 5 minutes per side until they turn deep golden brown
- Drain them on paper towels and repeat the process for all the egg rolls
- Take a blender and add avocado, cilantro, ranch dressing, and salt and pepper and blend it till you get a smooth mixture.
- Now cut the egg rolls in half and serve with the avocado ranch sauce

Mexican Shrimp Bites

If we spoke about a recipe that could be ready in less than 10 minutes and tastes so good that you would have all your guests drooling, won't you get super excited? Well, this is the one to keep an eye out for.

Ingredients

- 18 small to midsized shrimps
- 18 Lay's classic potato chips
- 2 tsp of olive oil
- ½ tsp of chili powder
- ¾ cup of guacamole
- Chopped cilantro for garnishing

Instructions

- Take a large pan and add olive oil to it and put it over a high flame
- Sprinkle chili powder over the shrimp
- Now take the shrimp and place it on the pan and cook it well
- Make sure to stir occasionally for 2 to 3 minutes until you find that they have turned pink
- Place 18 potato chips in a clean patter
- Spoon 2 tsp of guacamole on each one of the chips and then add a shrimp at the top
- Serve with cilantro

Chicken Chimichanga Boats

This isn't the most conventional choice of an appetizer and we do agree that not everyone loves chimichangas; nonetheless, it is surely a great option for a different appetizer which will have people complimenting you for your unique approach.

Ingredients

For the Chicken

- 4 boneless skinless chicken thighs
- 2 finely chopped chipotle peppers in adobo
- 1/2 tsp of dried oregano
- 1 tsp of ground cumin
- 1 tsp of garlic powder
- 1/2 tsp of black pepper
- 1 tbsp of vegetable oil

For the Boats

- Old El Paso Mini Soft Tortilla Taco Boats
- Warmed refried beans
- Sliced green onions
- Chopped tomatoes
- Shredded iceberg lettuce
- Freshly shredded cheddar cheese
- Guacamole
- Sour cream

Instructions

- Take a small bowl and add the vegetable oil along with garlic powder, chipotle peppers in adobo, oregano, black pepper, and cumin and mix well to combine thoroughly
- Now take a large zip-top plastic bag and place the chicken in it
- Add marinade to it and keep it in the fridge for a couple of hours
- Now take a grill and heat it to 400 degrees F
- Place the chicken on it and grill it for 5 minutes per side
- Now take off the chicken from the grill and let it rest for 10 minutes
- Chop it into small bite-sized pieces and keep aside

For the tacos

- Deep fry the taco boats
- Now remove it from the oil and let it sit on a paper towel to drain
- Now take a few tbsp of refried beans and place it on the bottom of the boat
- Top it with shredded lettuce along with a few pieces of the cooked chicken and all the toppings you have chosen for the taco
- Serve

Chapter 4: Mexican Breakfast Recipes

The Mexicans truly know how to hog on a breakfast right. Here, we are going to share some of the best breakfast recipes which will kick start your day on a high note and give you something to be really happy and cheerful about. After all, don't we say a happy meal makes for a happy heart?

Mexican Rice With Poached Eggs

There are few things as good as having the perfect Mexican rice for breakfast. If you can team it with poached eggs, the combination gets even better.

Ingredients

- 6 large eggs
- 1 pound of pork sausage; bulk and spicy
- 1 to 2 jalapeno peppers; seeded and minced
- 1 diced midsized onion
- 1 cup of long-grain rice; uncooked
- 1 diced midsized sweet red pepper
- 2 cloves of minced garlic
- 1 cup of shredded cheddar cheese
- 1 tbsp of beef base
- 2 cups of water
- 2 tsp of ground cumin
- 1 tsp of pepper

Instructions

- Take a Dutch oven and place it on sodium flame. Now cook sausage on it and add the crumbling piece of meat along with onion and peppers.
- Add garlic to it and cook for 1 more minute
- Stir the beef base along with the cumin and black pepper
- Add rice and then pour the water. Bring it to boil and let it simmer over low flame till the rice gets tender. Transfer it to a plate and let it stay warm
- Now take the eggs and poach them. For this, take 2 to cups of water in a skillet and boil it. Break the cold eggs and slip them into water.
- Cook them uncovered till the yolk thickens.
- Now take the eggs out of the water and place it on the rice and sprinkle it with cheese
- Serve

Easy Skillet Chicken Chilaquiles

With a cooking time of fewer than 30 minutes, this is another great dish to start your day. It could be a little heavy for breakfast which means that it goes well with brunch or even if you desire to skip lunch.

Ingredients

- 4 cup of rotisserie chicken; shredded
- 1 jar of green enchilada sauce (16 oz)
- 10 ounces of corn tortilla chips
- 1 cup of chicken broth; low sodium
- Salt and pepper to taste

Instructions

- Preheat the oven to 350 degrees F
- Take a large skillet and put to medium-high fame
- Now add the green enchilada sauce along with the chicken broth and bring the whole mix to boil. Reduce the flame a little and let it cook, making sure to mix occasionally
- Season it with the right amount for salt and pepper
- Now add tortilla chips to the skillet and stir them to coat evenly
- Add the shredded piece so chicken to the very top of the chips but make sure to leave a gap at the edges
- Keep the whole skillet in the oven for 20 minutes approx
- Serve it with whatever garnishing you want

Mexican Breakfast Casserole With Hash Brown Crust

Who doesn't love a good smoking hot pot of Mexican casserole? This dish might take over an hour to cook but it is something you are surely bound to savor and relish as every bite is worth it!

Ingredients

- 1 thawed shredded potatoes; 20-ounce bag
- 10 large eggs
- 1 diced red bell pepper
- ½ cup of chopped onions
- half of the milk
- 1 14-ounce can have drained and rinsed black beans
- 1 4-ounce can have diced and drained green chilies
- 2 tbsp of chopped cilantro + more for serving
- 1 ½ cups of shredded cheese
- ¼ cup of hot sauce
- 1 tbsp of taco seasoning
- 2 tbsp of melted butter or oil
- 2 tsp of oil

Instructions

- Take a midsized skillet and put it over medium to high flame
- Add 2 tsp of oil and then sauté onions in it for 2 minutes
- Move them to a fresh bowl and allow it to cool
- Now take a baking dish and add cooking spray to it
- Take a rack and keep it in the center of the oven and put it to preheat by raising the temperature to 375 degrees F
- Now take another fresh large bowl and whisk the eggs along with half and a half and add sauce to this
- Add ½ tsp of salt and the same amount of black pepper.
- Add the bell peppers along with cooked onions, green chilies, black beans, cheese, as well as cilantro and put this whole mix on the baking dish
- Take a midsized bowl and add the shredded potatoes to it along with taco seasoning
- Drizzle melted butter on top of it and mix well to make sure the potatoes are well coated
- Sprinkle this shredded potatoes all over the egg mix
- Bake the whole casserole keeping it uncovered for an hour till the hash browns are done
- Let it cool for 10 minutes
- Serve with chopped cilantro and a dip of your choice

Chapter 5: Mexican Lunch Recipes

Now that we are done with the first meal of the day, let us shift our focus on lunch. Mexican lunch is mostly known to be a lavish affair because the Mexicans have no qualms about eating. So, here we're going to share some of the most amazing recipes for you which you can devour during your lunchtime and be satiated with your appetite.

Mexican Chicken Lunch Bowls

When you are wondering what to make for lunch, making a scrumptious lunch bowl might sound like a cool idea. This recipe will guide you exactly how!

Ingredients

- 4 chicken breast
- 1 tsp of ground coriander
- 2-3 tbsp of lime juice
- 3 tbsp of olive oil
- 1-2 tbsp of chipotle powder
- 1 tsp of ground cumin
- 2 tsp of salt
- 1 tsp of pepper

For the quinoa and bulgur wheat

- ¾ cup of quinoa
- ¾ cup of bulgur wheat
- 3 cups of water
- 1 tsp of salt

For the lunch bowls

- 2 cups of halved cherry tomatoes
- 2 cups of sweet corn
- 1 sliced avocado
- Lime wedges for serving
- Salt and pepper as per taste

Instructions

- Take all the ingredients for the marinade and mix them well
- Pour it over the chicken and let it marinate overnight
- Now take a saucepan and add bulgur wheat and quinoa to it along with water and salt. Bring the whole thing to boil and keep it on low flame
- Allow it to simmer for 20 minutes and then cover it with a lid and cut off the flame
- Now take a non-stick frying pan and put it on medium flame. Cook chicken on it till it turns golden brown. Allow it to rest
- Now add sweet corn to the pan and let it cook for 5 minutes
- Slice the chicken and serve it over the grains along with charred corn, avocados, and sliced tomatoes

Vegan Black Bean Burgers

If you are a foodie and would love to have a loaded burger for lunch, this is one of the winning recipes you need to ace.

Ingredients

- 2 midsized sweet potatoes; halved
- 1/2 cup dry quinoa (about 1 1/2 cups cooked)
- 1 15-ounce can black beans, drained and rinsed
- 1 tsp of onion powder
- 3 tbsp of ground flax seed
- 2 tsp of ground cumin
- 1/2 tsp of garlic powder
- 1/4 tsp of dried oregano
- 1 tsp of coarse kosher salt
- 1/4 tsp of ground black pepper
- 1 tsp of chili powder
- Olive oil

Instructions

- Preheat the oven to 400 degrees F
- Now take a large baking sheet and line it with aluminum foil and spray with nonstick cooking spray
- Place the sweet potatoes that have been halved on it. Make sure that the cut side is down. Poke every half with a fork 4 to 5 times.
- Bake it for half an hour till the potatoes turn tender and have cooked well. Remove them from the oven and let it cool for some time
- Now take a sieve and rinse the quinoa in it by running it under cool water
- Drain it and transfer to a midsized pot
- Add a cup of water and boil it over a high flame
- Now turn the heat to low, cover the pot and let it simmer for 10 to 15 minutes till the quinoa cooks through completely
- Let it stand for 5 minutes and then remove the lid and fluff it with the help of a fork
- Now take a small fresh bowl and add ground flax seed along with kosher salt, black pepper, ground cumin, garlic powder, and onion powder and oregano. Mix well and keep aside
- Take another bowl and add the black beans along with the cooked wet potatoes. Mash them till you get a good consistency.
- Now add the quinoa that was cooked along with the spices. Mix everything till the mixture seems uniform

- Take this mixture and form 8 burger patties, each of which should contain nearly 1/3 cup of the mixture
- Now take a large baking sheet that is lined with parchment paper and place the burger patties and bake them for 20 minutes at 400 degrees F
- Flip them and bake for the next 20 minutes
- Remove from oven
- Serve

Cilantro Lime Rice

The taste of cilantro is known to each one of us and Mexicans love to use its flavor in a lot of things. This rice recipe is hands down a clear winner.

Ingredients

- 1 cup of rinsed wet rice; long-grained
- ¼ cup of cilantro; chopped
- 2 cups of chicken broth
- 1 zested and juiced lime
- 2 tbsp of warm water
- ½ tsp of salt

Instructions

- Take a deep skillet and put it over to medium to high flame and add the broth to it. Bring it to boil
- Now add in the rice and salt. Turn the heat to low, cover the pot and let it cook for 15 or 20 minutes till the rice has been cooked and the water has been completely absorbed
- Now remove the rice from the heat source and let it stand for some time
- Fluff it with the help of a fork
- Add cilantro, lime juice, lime zest, and water
- Mix well and serve hot

Low Carb Taco Bowls

If you are on a keto diet or you are very calorie-conscious and want to opt for a low carb healthy diet, this lunch bowl is surely the right pick for you. It will be prepared easily and that too in less than 30 minutes, so, are we good to go?

Ingredients

For the meat:

- 1 lb of ground beef
- 2 tsp of apple cider vinegar
- 2 tbsp of tomato paste

For the taco bowls:

- 1-2 chopped bell pepper
- Cauliflower rice
- 1/2 cup of grape tomatoes
- 1 small zucchini; sliced into thin halves
- 1/2 cup of cabbage; green & red, shredded
- Avocado slices
- Olive slices
- Lime wedges

For the homemade taco seasoning:

- 1/2 tsp of garlic powder
- 1/4 tsp of oregano
- 1 tsp of cumin
- 1/2 tsp of onion powder
- 1 tsp of sea salt
- 1/4 tsp of paprika
- 2 tsp of chili powder

- 1/4 tsp of black pepper

Instructions

- Take a small-sized bowl and add all the spices for the taco seasoning
- Now take a large skillet and place it on medium to high heat
- Cook ground meat in it and make sure to slowly break it into small pieces when it is being cooked
- After approximately 3 minutes, add 1 tbsp of taco seasoning to it and continue to cook till the meat has completely cooked
- Now mix the tomato paste and vinegar and then cook for a couple of more minutes
- Add seasoning as needed

For the bowls

- Divide the cauliflower rice amongst the bowls
- Top it with a generous serving of cooked meat along with shredded cabbage, bell peppers, olive, tomatoes, avocados, and lime wedges
- Add taco toppings as per need
- Serve

Chapter 6: Mexican Dinner Recipes

Now we are headed to the fine meal segment for the day. Dinner could be scrumptious, lavish or alternately some people prefer to keep to light as they head to their bed to take a long nap after dinner. This is why we are going to offer you a mix of all types so that you can choose based on what you deem to be most suited for your lifestyle, and body.

Tarragon Rubbed Salmon

For those who love to have salmon for dinner, this typical icon dish when prepared with the finest salsa is sure to leave you craving for one round more!

Ingredients

- 4 pieces of salmon fillet; skinless
- 1 small red pepper
- 1 jalapeno chile
- 2 large nectarines; ripe
- 2 tbsp of fresh lime juice
- 1 tbsp of dried tarragon
- 2 tbsp of red onion; chopped
- 1 tbsp of chopped cilantro; fresh
- 1 tsp of olive oil
- ½ tsp of salt
- ¼ tsp of ground black pepper

Instructions

- Grease the grates of the grill and prepare it for covered and direct grilling by preheating it
- Now take a fresh bowl and add the chopped red onions in it. Cover it with water and allow it to sit for 10 minutes
- Take another bowl and add nectarines along with jalapeño which is finely chopped, cilantro, red pepper, lime juice and ¼ tsp of salt and keep it aside. They will help in making the salsa
- Now take another bowl and add tarragon along with ¼ tsp of salt and ¼ tsp of ground black pepper
- Take the salmon and brush it with oil and rub the tarragon mixture to coat on both the sides
- Place the coated salmon on the hot grill grate, cover it and cook for 10 minutes approx while making sure to turn it once in between. The salmon should turn opaque
- Now drain the onion well and stir it well in the nectarine mixture.
- Serve salmon with nectarine salsa

Turkey Tacos

When mentioning Mexican recipe, the taco has to feature in just about every meal of the day, isn't it? This is another amazing recipe to have a great dinner which will leave everyone happy and satisfied.

Ingredients

- 1 lb of ground turkey
- 8 warmed hard corn taco shells
- 1 finely chopped large onion, plus more for serving
- 1/2 cup of canned tomato sauce
- 1/2 cup of grated cheddar cheese
- 1/4 cup of roughly chopped fresh cilantro leaves
- 1/2 small head of shredded iceberg lettuce
- 2 cloves of pressed garlic
- 1 tsp of ground cumin
- ½ to 1 ½ tsp of chipotle Chile powder
- 1 tbsp of olive oil
- Kosher salt
- Sour cream and lime wedges, for serving

Instructions

- Take a large skillet and heat oil in it over medium flame
- Now add onion along with ¼ tsp of salt and cook it while covering the lid, make sure to stir occasionally. Do so for 6 to 8 minutes till they turn tender
- Mix garlic and cook for an additional minute
- Now add turkey and cook it. Make it a point to break it into small pieces. Continue cooking for 5 minutes
- Add chipotle powder along with cumin and ½ tsp of salt and cook for 2 more minutes while still breaking the turkey
- Now add in the tomato sauce and let it simmer for 5 minutes till the whole thing starts to thicken
- Now take a bowl and toss lettuce along with cilantro.
- Take the taco shells and fill it with turkey and then top it with cheddar cheese followed by lettuce
- Serve it with onion, sour cream, and lime wedges

Chicken, Sausage And White Bean Stew

Many of us prefer to have some stew before heading to bed as it seems like a much better choice. If you too are in for stew, this is by far one of the perfect recipes for you to try your hands on!

Ingredients

- 8 chicken thighs (2 1/4 pounds each)
- 1 lb of sweet Italian sausage (about 5 links)
- 2 cup of low-sodium chicken broth
- 1/2 lb of bacon, cut into 1/2-inch pieces
- 2 cup of fresh breadcrumbs (about 5 ounces)
- 1 medium onion, finely chopped
- 2 15-ounce cans of rinsed cannellini beans
- 2 medium finely chopped carrots
- 1 stalk of finely chopped celery
- 2 cloves of pressed garlic
- 2 tbsp of fresh thyme leaves
- 1 tbsp of olive oil
- Kosher salt and pepper

Instructions

- Heat the oven to 350 degrees F
- Take a Dutch oven and heat oil in it over medium flame
- Pat the chicken dry and then season it with the appropriate amount of salt and pepper
- Now make sure to keep the skin side facing downwards in the pan and cook it till it has turned golden brown. This should take approx 5 minutes
- Turn and flip it and cook for 2 more minutes. Later, move to a plate
- Now take a pot and add sausages to it and cook it till it has turned brown. This should take 5 to 7 minutes
- Transfer to a cutting board and let into cool for a while and then slice it evenly
- Now add bacon to the pot and cook. Make sure to stir it occasionally until it turns golden brown and becomes crisp.
- Take a spoon and transfer it slowly to clean paper towels and discard all except 2 tbsp of fat in the pot
- Add onions along with ¼ tsp of salt to the pot and let it cook. Do not forget to keep stirring. Let it cook for 5 minutes
- Now add carrots and celery and let it cook for 3 more minutes after which remove the pot from the flame
- Now take a fresh small bowl and add breadcrumbs along with garlic and thyme and keep it aside

- Mix beans and broth in the pot along with the chicken, bacon, and sausage and sprinkle the breadcrumb mixture all over it
- Bake the whole thing till the chicken becomes fork-tender and the stew has thickened
- Now heat the broiler and broil it well till the crumbs turn golden brown
- Let it stand for 10 minutes and cool
- Serve

Taco Lasagna

Yes, you read it right, the taco has featured once again in our recipe list because there is no such thing as too many tacos, right? Let us go for it!

Ingredients

- 1 pound of ground beef
- 6 flour tortillas (8 inches)
- 1 can (16 ounces) of refried beans
- 1 can (15 ounces) of rinsed and drained black beans
- 1/2 cup of chopped green pepper
- 1 can (14-1/2 ounces) of undrained Mexican diced tomatoes
- 1/2 cup of chopped onion
- 1 envelope taco seasoning
- 3 cups of shredded Mexican cheese blend
- 2/3 cup of water

Instructions

- Take a large skillet and cook the beef in it. Add both green pepper and onion and heat it over medium flame till the meat doesn't look pink anymore
- Add water and taco seasoning to it and bring it to boil
- Now reduce the heat and let it simmer while leaving it uncovered for a couple of minutes
- Add in the black beans along with tomatoes and let it simmer in the uncovered state for 10 more minutes
- Now take 2 tortillas and place it in a baking dish that has been thoroughly greased
- Spread half of the refried beans along with half of the beef mixture on it
- Sprinkle a cup of cheese on it
- Repeat the layering and top it with the leftover tortillas and cheese
- Cover it and then let it bake at 350 degrees for half an hour
- Serve

Creamy Salmon Chowder

If you are the kind of person who likes to have chowder soup kind of thing for dinner, this recipe is the one you need to ace. It is great to keep yourself warm during the winters and feel cozy, light, and comfortable as well. Don't forget; it is creamy enough to feel every bit Mexican!

Ingredients

- 3/4 lb of skinless salmon filet
- 1 bunch of scallions
- 1 lb of red potatoes
- 2 cup of frozen corn
- 2 tbsp of flour
- 1 qt. nonfat milk
- 1 stalk of celery
- 3 cloves of garlic
- 1 tsp of crushed red pepper flakes
- 1/2 tsp of dried thyme
- Chopped fresh dill
- 1 tbsp of olive oil
- Kosher salt
- Pepper

Instructions

- Take a Dutch oven and heat oil in it over medium flame
- Add scallions along with thyme, celery, garlic, red pepper, and salt and let it cook for 5 minutes. Make sure to stir occasionally
- Now sprinkle the mixture with flour and cook for an additional minute making sure to stir all the while
- Add the milk along with a cup of water and stir well
- Now add potatoes and allow it to simmer for 5 minutes
- Add both salmon and corn and allow it to cook or 3 to 5 minutes until the salmon has turned opaque
- Top with fresh dill
- Serve

Mini Chicken Meatballs With Crispy Potatoes

Meatballs happen to be a perennial favorite among everyone and this recipe is no different. With a net cooking time of 20 minutes, it is a great idea for those quick recipes that need little or no fixing.

Ingredients

- 2 eggs
- 2 lb of ground chicken
- 1 cup of breadcrumbs
- 4 cloves of garlic; minced
- 1 cup of finely grated parmesan cheese
- A pinch of dried oregano
- 1 ½ tsp of salt
- ¼ cup of olive oil; extra for frying
- 1 ½ lb of baby golden Yukon potatoes
- Romesco sauce
- Salt to taste

Instructions

- Take all ingredients except the baby golden potatoes and Romesco sauce in a large bowl and mix it well
- Roll them into small bite-sized balls and place it on a clean baking sheet
- Now take a large skillet and heat some olive oil in it over medium flame
- Add meatballs in small batches and make sure to flip them every few minutes. Cook well till the inside has cooked thoroughly
- Now take the same pan and fry the potatoes for 10 minutes using a little more olive oil and salt
- Serve the meatballs with the potatoes and the Romesco sauce

Chipotle Orange Glazed Salmon

Yet another salmon dish which you need to learn the art of cooking. This comes with its typical Mexican flavor and the orange glaze is likely to have everyone hooked to it in no time.

Ingredients

- 4 piece of skinless salmon fillet
- 1 bunch of radish
- 1 orange
- 2 green onions
- 1/2 cup of fresh corn kernels
- 1 cup of quinoa
- 1 clove of garlic
- 1 chipotle Chile in adobo sauce
- 2 tsp of adobo sauce (from chipotle chilies)
- 1/2 tsp of ground cumin
- 1/2 cup of fresh cilantro leaves
- Salt as per taste

Instructions

- Place the oven rack at least 4 to 6 inches away from the broiler heat source
- Preheat the broiler on high flame
- Now line the jelly roll pan with foil
- Prepare quinoa as per the directions on the package and when done, transfer it to a clean, fresh bowl
- Now take the orange and grate 1 tsp of peel from it and squeeze ½ cup for juice
- Take a blender and puree the chipotle along with adobo sauce, cumin, orange juice, and garlic
- To the bowl containing quinoa, add radish along with green onion, corn, orange peel, cilantro and 1/8 tsp of salt
- Now arrange the salmon on the pan you had prepared before.
- Sprinkle 1/8 tsp of salt again and brush it on all sides along with the Chile mixture
- Broil the whole thing for 5 to 7 minutes till it has turned opaque
- Serve the salmon on quinoa pilaf

Chapter 7: Mexican Soup Recipes

The perfect taste of the Mexican soup is something to die for. In this chapter, we are going to share some of the winning recipes as far as Mexican soups are concerned. Make sure to have them either for breakfast or even for your dinner.

Mexican Vegetable Soup

Let us start with something typically Mexican and common but popular. This take on the regular vegetable soup is different because the Mexican flavors have been infused to it.

Ingredients

- 5 cups of low-sodium vegetable broth
- 1 ½ cups of chopped yellow onion (1 medium)
- 6 oz diced green beans (1 1/4 cups)
- 1 diced red bell pepper
- 1 medium chopped zucchini (1 3/4 cups)
- 1 cup of peeled and diced carrots (2 medium)
- 1 ½ (14.5 oz) can of diced tomatoes with green chilies
- 1 ¾ cups of frozen corn or drained and rinsed canned hominy
- ½ cup of chopped cilantro
- 2 cloves of minced garlic
- 1 tsp of dried oregano
- 1 tsp of ground cumin
- 1 1/2 tbsp of olive oil
- 2 tbsp of fresh lime juice
- Salt and freshly ground black pepper

Instructions

- Take a large pot and put it over medium to high flame
- Heat olive oil in it
- Add onions along with carrot and sauté it for 3 minutes approx
- Now add garlic to it and sauté it for one minute
- Add in the vegetable broth along with zucchini, bell pepper, tomatoes, green beans, cumin, oregano, and salt and pepper as per taste
- Bring the whole thing to boil and then turn down the heat to medium-low
- Cover it and simmer it till the vegetables turn soft
- Stir corn along with lime juice and cilantro and cook it well till you feel that the corn has thoroughly heated
- Serve warm

Mexican Chicken Corn Chowder

The combination of chicken and corn is sure to be a real winner. When you are looking for an excellent soup recipe which could also double up as a dinner; this seems like a good option for you.

Ingredients

- 1 ½ pound of boneless skinless chicken breasts, cut into 1-inch pieces
- 1 medium chopped tomato
- ½ cup of chopped onion
- 1 can (14-3/4 ounces) of cream-style corn
- 1 can (4 ounces) of undrained chopped green chiles
- 2 tsp of chicken bouillon granules
- 3 tbsp of butter
- 2 cups half-and-half cream
- 1 cup of hot water
- 2 cups of shredded Monterey Jack cheese
- 1 to 2 minced garlic cloves
- ½ to 1 tsp of ground cumin
- ¼ to 1 tsp of hot pepper sauce

Instructions

- Take a Dutch oven and add the chicken and onion in it while adding butter to it.
- Cook it till the chicken is no longer pinkish
- Now add garlic to the mix and cook for one more minute
- Add water along with cumin and bouillon and bring the whole thing to boil
- Reduce the heat flame and cover the whole thing and let it simmer for 5 minutes
- Now add the cream along with corn, cheese, hot pepper sauce, and chiles
- Cook on low flame and make sure to stir it continuously
- Add tomato in between
- Serve hot

Black Bean And Almond Soup

This is another great eclectic combination that is sure to help you relish the perfect taste of the soup. It is easy to make this recipe and the rich taste means that people will love to gobble it.

Ingredients

- 4 cups of chicken broth
- 2 cup of finely chopped red onion
- 2 cans of drained and rinsed black beans; 15 ounces each
- 4 cloves of chopped garlic
- 2 tbsp of extra virgin olive oil
- ½ tsp of ground cumin
- ¼ cup of sliced almonds; more for serving
- ½ cup of fresh cilantro leaves; more for serving
- Sliced avocado for serving
- Plain Greek yogurt for serving
- Coarse salt and freshly ground pepper as per taste

Instructions

- Take a medium-sized pot and heat oil in it over medium flame
- Add 1 ½ cups of onion and season it with salt and pepper and cook well for 8 to 10 minutes approx, making sure to stir it in between
- Now add garlic and cumin to it and cook well while stirring in between
- Add both beans and broth and bring the whole mixture to boil
- Reduce the heat and let it simmer until the beans have heated thoroughly and they turn creamy. It should take about 10 minutes
- Let it cool a little
- Now while working in batches; transfer the soup to a blender and then add cilantro and almonds
- Pulse them well until beans have been chopped. Make sure not to puree them
- Season it with salt and pepper
- Divide the soup into bowls and serve with ½ cup of onion along with almonds, avocado, yogurt, and cilantro

Mexican Corn And Poblano Soup

This is another great combination of soup which is both healthy and delicious. No doubt, preparing it is also easy and so you can have a quick recipe at your hands.

Ingredients

- 1 white onion; quartered lengthwise
- 3 scallions
- 1 ½ pound of frozen corn kernels; thawed and drained
- 2 poblano chiles; large and fresh
- 2 tbsp of fine cornmeal
- 1 tbsp of salt
- 4 cups plus 3 tbsp of water
- Crumbled queso fresco cheese

Instructions

- Take the scallions and cut the dark green tops off and chop it finely
- Take a large skillet and put in on medium to high flame
- Now add scallions, chiles, and onion in it and cook it undisturbed for 5 minutes
- Turn in the vegetables and cook undisturbed on the other side for 5 more minutes
- Now transfer the scallions to a blender
- Make sure to turn and char the chiles and onion thoroughly
- Remove the skillet from the heat source and transfer the onion to the blender
- Now take the chiles and move them to a bowl
- Cover it with a plastic wrap and steam it for 15 minutes
- Peel and discard the charred skin from the chiles and also get rid of the stem and seeds
- Half the chiles lengthwise and also slice them in a way that you have ¼ inch thick strips
- Now add 2 ½ cups of corn along with salt and 2 cups of water to a blender and puree it till you get a smooth mix
- Transfer this puree to a skillet and add in the leftover corn along with 2 cups of water
- Bring it to boil over a high flame
- Now reduce the heat and let it simmer making sure to stir occasionally

- Whisk the cornmeal along with 3 tbsp of water and stir it in the soup along with the chiles and let it simmer
- Serve with chopped scallion greens and cheese

Mexican Meatball Soup

This soup is packed with some of the healthiest ingredients you can think of. It is a fun soup and can be a great way to fill up your appetite without adding up on too many calories as well.

Ingredients

- 1 large egg
- 1 ½ pound of ground beef
- 6 cups of low sodium chicken broth
- 1 midsized chopped yellow onion
- 1 large zucchini
- 1/3 cup of uncooked long-grain white rice
- 2 cups of packed baby spinach
- ½ cup of fresh mint; finely chopped
- ¼ cup of fresh cilantro; finely chopped
- 1 can of 15-ounce tomato sauce
- 2 tbsp of extra virgin olive oil
- ½ tsp of ground cinnamon
- Salt and black pepper as per taste

Instructions

- Take a large bowl and mix beef, along with cilantro, egg, rice, salt, pepper, cinnamon and mint.
- Now form meatballs out of it by scooping the mixture out of it and shaping it well
- Take a large pot and heat oil over a medium-high flame
- Now add onions and cook it for 3 minutes until they turn soft
- Now add broth along with 2 cups of water, zucchini meatballs, and tomato sauce
- Simmer it on medium heat for half an hour until they have cooked thoroughly
- Season it with salt and pepper
- Mix spinach and then serve it while topping it with cilantro leaves

Chapter 8: Mexican Sauce Recipes

Like we have told before, Mexican cuisine is all about getting the sauces and flavors right. In this chapter, we are going to focus on some of the typical Mexican sauces and how to get the perfection in them. Almost all dishes become doubly amazing when paired with the right dip.

Red Enchilada Sauce

This is one of the best sauces which is infused with the perfect kind of flavor that is sure to make any recipe wonderful. The fact that it is easy to make and can be stored and used later is another reason why you need to stock up on it.

Ingredients

- 1 can of tomato sauce; 6 ounce
- 2 cloves of minced garlic
- ¼ cup of salsa
- 1 ½ cup of water
- 1 tsp of minced onion
- ½ tsp of dried oregano
- ½ tsp of dried basil
- 1 tsp of dried parsley
- ¼ tsp of ground cumin
- 2 ½ tsp of chili powder
- 1 tbsp of olive oil
- 1/8 tsp of salt
- 1/8 tsp of ground black pepper

Instructions

- Take a large saucepan and heat it over medium flame
- Add garlic and sauté it for a couple of minutes
- Now add onion, chili powder, cumin, oregano, parsley, basil, salsa, ground black pepper, salt, and tomato sauce
- Mix everything and stir it in water
- Bring it to boil and reduce the heat to low and simmer it for 15 to 20 minutes
- Serve

Pico de Gallo

This salsa is known by a lot of different names and it is one of the very popular ones in the whole of Mexico. Make sure not to stock it for too long as it should be consumed within 2 days.

Ingredients

- 2 cups of chopped and seeded ripe tomatoes
- ½ chopped onion
- Bunch of fresh cilantro leaves chopped
- 1 tbsp of lime juice
- 6 cloves of finely chopped fresh garlic
- ½ tsp of salt
- 1 finely chopped jalapeno pepper

Instructions

- Take a handful of cilantro leaves and pull them out so that you can get firm leaves
- Mix all the ingredients until they have all been incorporated well
- Serve immediately

Ranchera Sauce

The Ranchera sauce enjoys a great deal of popularity in Mexican cuisine. It can be made in less than 30 minutes and tastes delicious and has the typical Mexican flavor.

Ingredients

- ¼ cup of chopped onion
- 3 cups of peeled and diced fresh tomatoes
- 2 tbsp of vegetable oil
- 2 cloves of diced garlic
- 1 tbsp of dried oregano
- 1 seeded and diced jalapeno chile
- Salt to taste

Instructions

- Take a medium-sized saucepan and put it over medium to high flame
- Add onions along with garlic and fresh chile pepper and sauté it for a couple of minutes. Make sure to mix occasionally to ensure that the ingredients do to turn brown
- Now lower the heat to medium-low and then add tomatoes and cook for 5 minutes till they become soft. Make sure to stir in between
- Now add oregano and salt as per taste and simmer it for 5 more minutes
- If required, let it cool and pulse it in a blender to get a smoother mix. You can also use as it is based on your preferences

Salsa Taqueria

This is a fiery salsa sauce which is made using tomatoes and Arbol chiles. If you have a thing for spicy food and want to make the most of the Mexican dip, this recipe is surely the best one to choose from.

It is prepared in less than 10 minutes and is amazingly tasty.

Ingredients

- 2 plum tomatoes
- 6 dried Arbol chiles
- 1 white onion
- 6 tbsp of cooking oil
- 3 cloves of garlic
- ½ tsp of salt, plus more to taste as per need

Instructions

- Take the tomatoes and chop them roughly along with onion
- Peel the cloves of garlic and remove the stem from the Arbol pepper
- Preheat the pan and add 2 tbsp of cooking oil over medium heat
- Add chopped tomatoes and onion and cook it for 5 minutes and stir it occasionally
- Add garlic to the pan and cook it for 2 minutes
- Now add Arbol peppers and cook for 1 more minute
- Blend all the ingredients for salsa for half a minute
- When it is being blended, add4 tbsp of cooking oil and blend for an additional minute until the salsa gets thick and shiny
- Season it with salt and taste it
- Serve

Creamy Avocado Salsa

This is another great salsa sauce that is infused with the perfect flavors and has a pleasant tangy taste to it. This salsa is also kid-friendly and can help in making any meal much more delicious.

Another bonus tip here is that serve it along with tostadas and it is sure to increase the taste by leaps and bounds.

Ingredients

- 3 tomatillos
- 3 ripe avocados
- 4 tbsp of sour cream
- 1 clove of garlic
- 6 tbsp of water
- 1 tsp of salt
- 1 serrano chile

Instructions

- Pit the avocados and remove the flesh out of it
- Now take the tomatillos and peel it thoroughly and wash it well
- Also, remove the stems from the Serrano chile
- Peel the cloves of garlic and also squeeze the juice from a lime
- Add all the leftover ingredients in a blender and blend it thoroughly
- Add water to it; if you feel that the salsa has thickened, but, make sure to do it 2 tbsp at a time
- Chill the salsa for an hour
- Add salt as necessary

Chapter 9: Mexican Salad

Now that we are done with sauces, we want to shift our focus on to salads. We all know that salads are by far one of the healthiest options and it is important to ensure that your body gets the right dose of nutrients and vitamins. The good thing about Mexican salads is that they tend to infuse the right flavor which makes even a bowl of salad all the more delicious.

Mexican Bean Salad

This is a spicy and refreshing salad which can be a great way to load up your appetite and stock your body with the right dose of minerals and more.

Ingredients

- 1 can of rinsed and drained black beans; 15 ounce
- 1 can of rinsed and drained cannellini beans; 15 ounce
- 1 can of drained kidney beans; 15 ounce
- 1 package of 10 ounces of frozen corn kernels
- 1 chopped red bell pepper
- 1 chopped green bell pepper
- 1 chopped red onion
- 1 clove of crushed garlic
- ¼ cup of fresh cilantro; chopped
- ½ cup of red wine vinegar
- 2 tbsp of fresh lime juice
- 1 tbsp of lemon juice
- ½ cup of olive oil
- 2 tbsp of white sugar
- ½ tbsp of ground cumin
- 1 tbsp of salt
- ½ tbsp of ground black pepper
- 1 dash of hot pepper sauce
- ½ tsp of chili powder

Instructions

- Take a large bowl and add beans along with frozen corn, bell peppers, and onion to it
- Now take another bowl and whisk the leftover ingredients except for hot sauce and chili powder. Add these later as a seasoning
- Now pour the olive oil dressing over the vegetable and mix it well
- Chill thoroughly and serve cold for the best taste

Quick Taco Salad

Yes, you got it right, even when we are talking of salad; there is a taco in here. This is precisely how much the Mexicans love their tacos.

Ingredients

- 2 pounds of ground beef chuck
- 1 chopped onion
- 1 cup of halved cherry tomatoes
- 1 bag of corn chips; 10.5 ounces
- ½ cup of chopped black olives
- 2 cups of shredded green leaf lettuce
- 2 cups of shredded cheddar
- 2 seeded and chopped jalapeno poppers
- 2 envelopes of taco seasoning mix
- 2 cups of salsa
- 1 cup of sour cream
- 1 ½ cup of water

Instructions

- Take a large skillet and put it over medium flame
- Add the ground beef to it and brown it. Make sure to allow the heat to crumble it into smaller pieces and then drain the excess grease present in it. This should take approximately 10 minutes
- Now add the taco seasoning along with water
- Bring the whole beef mixture to boil and cook till it has thickened
- Transfer the beef mixture to a separate bowl
- Now add the chopped onions along with tomatoes, black olives, lettuce, cheddar cheese, salsa, sour cream, corn chips, and jalapeño pepper
- Serve along with beef and make a scrumptious salad

Mexican Bean And Rice Salad

Now, it comes as no surprise that Mexicans love rice and salad. It has always been a great combination to go with rice. So, this recipe is another amazing combination that will load your appetite and keep you healthy at the same time.

Ingredients

- 2 cups of cooked brown rice
- 1 can of drained whole kernel corn; 15 ounce
- 1 can of rinsed and drained kidney beans; 15 ounce
- 1 can of rinsed and drained black beans; 15 ounce
- 1 diced green bell pepper
- 1 diced onion
- 1 zested and juiced lime
- 2 diced and seeded jalapeno peppers
- ¼ cup of cilantro leaves; chopped
- 1 ½ tsp of ground cumin
- 1 tsp of minced garlic
- Salt as per taste

Instructions

- Take a large bowl and add in all the ingredients in it
- Toss all of them to ensure that they have mixed well
- Sprinkle salt as per taste
- Refrigerate the whole thing for an hour
- Toss well again and serve

Jicama Salad With Cilantro And Lime

This salad could double up as a great side dish and it is very refreshing to have during summers. The taste of lime makes it all the better as the tanginess gives it the right twist.

Ingredients

- 2 pounds of peeled and julienned Jicama
- ¼ cup of lime juice
- ¼ cup of cilantro leaves; chopped
- Salt and pepper as per taste

Instructions

- Take a large bowl and add all the ingredients to it except the lime juice. Mix them well
- Sprinkle lime juice on top and coat it evenly
- Refrigerate and serve cold when needed

Super Tex-Mex Chicken Chop Salad

This is a heavy dish that you can gobble up for dinner and then skip any other meal altogether. It is great as far as the health rating is concerned. At the same time, it is easy to cook and looks yum too!

Ingredients

- 1 whole skinless, boneless chicken breast; halved
- ½ head of chopped iceberg lettuce
- ½ green bell pepper; well cut into cubes measuring ¼ inches each
- 1 chopped tomato
- ¼ cup of jalapeno peppers; seeded and chopped
- ¼ cup of drained and sliced black olives
- ¼ cup of canned corn kernels; drained
- ¼ cup of black beans; rinsed and drained
- 2 tbsp of butter
- 2 tbsp of green chile peppers; chopped
- 2 tbsp of steak seasoning
- ½ cup of shredded cheddar cheese
- ¼ tsp of garlic powder
- 1 cup of ranch dressing
- ½ tsp of ground black pepper

Instructions

- Take the chicken breast and sprinkle the steak seasoning evenly over it
- Now take a frying pan and put it over medium flame
- Melt butter in it and cook chicken till it is no longer pinkish. This should take approx 5 to 10 minutes per side
- Now remove the chicken from the heated pan and then cut it into small sized pieces
- Take a fresh large bowl and add lettuce along with tomato, bell pepper, chicken, black olives, jalapeno pepper, corn, chile pepper, black beans, and cheese. Gently toss to make sure that they all mix well
- Now whisk the ranch dressing and use the reserved 3 tbsp of jalapeno juice along with garlic and black pepper in a fresh bowl
- Drizzle this seasoning all over the salad and toss well to coat thoroughly
- Serve

Chapter 10: Mexican Sweet And Desserts

What is a cookbook unless it has the recipe for some of the best savories; which includes sweets and desserts alike. The Mexicans love food and when it comes to treats, they are no different. If you explore the depth of the Mexican cuisine, you will find it to be filled with some of the most amazing desserts. Here, we are going to share some such winning recipes which will have everyone licking their fingers.

Rumchata Cheesecake

For all of you who love a little rum in your dessert, this cheesecake is sure to be a heaven's delight. It has a generous serving of rum and the flavor is so good that you won't be able to stop yourself from hogging it.

Ingredients

For the crust

- 9 finely crushed graham crackers (1 sleeve)
- 1/4 cup of granulated sugar
- 6 tbsp of melted butter
- 2 tsp of ground cinnamon
- Pinch kosher salt
- Cooking spray

For the filling

- 4 large eggs
- 4 (8-oz.) block of softened cream cheese
- 1/3 cup of RumChata liqueur
- 1 tsp of pure vanilla extract
- 3/4 cup of granulated sugar
- 3 tbsp of cornstarch
- 1/4 cup of packed brown sugar
- 1/2 tsp of ground cinnamon
- Pinch kosher salt

For the topping

- Cinnamon sugar
- Cool whip
- Caramel sauce

Instructions

- Preheat the oven to 325 degrees F and grease a pan with the help of cooking spray
- Now for making the crust, you need to take a large bowl and add the graham cracker crumbs to it.
- Along with this, add butter, salt, sugar, and cinnamon till it has mixed well
- Toss this at the very bottom of the pan and make sure to push the sides up. Now keep the whole thing aside
- Take a large bowl and use a hand mixer to beat the cream cheese along with sugar. Make sure that there are no visible lumps after that
- Now add the eggs and do this one at a time
- Mix vanilla and rumchata along with it
- Finally, add cornstarch, salt, and cinnamon and beat it well till it has combined thoroughly
- Pour this whole mixture over the crust
- Wrap the bottom of the pan with the help of aluminum foil and place it in the large roasting pan
- Now add enough boiling water to cover the pan midway
- Bake till the center of the cake begins to jiggle. This should take approximately 1.5 hours and then turn off the heat and take it out of the oven. Allow it to cool for an hour
- Remove the foil and refrigerate the cheesecake for a minimum of 5 hours. You can also keep it overnight as well

- Now spread the cool whip on the top of the cheesecake. Make sure to have a thick layer and then sprinkle cinnamon all over it
- Finally, drizzle caramel and serve

Mexican Hot Chocolate Pie

Every time someone mentions hot chocolate, you are bound to get a foodgasm. There is something about hot chocolate that makes it so endearing. If you can have it in the middle of frosty winters, things can't get any better.

Ingredients

For the crust

- 10 graham crackers
- 1/3 cup of granulated sugar
- 6 tbsp of melted butter
- Kosher salt
- Cooking spray, for a pie dish

For the pie

- 4 egg yolks
- 3 cup of whole milk
- 1/3 cup of cornstarch
- 2 tbsp of butter
- 3/4 cup of sugar
- 1 tsp of vanilla extract
- 1 1/2 tsp of cinnamon
- 2 cup of Hershey's Special Dark Chocolate Chips
- 1 tsp of salt
- 1/3 tsp of cayenne pepper

For the topping

- 1 cup of whipped topping
- 1 cup of marshmallow cream
- Chocolate shavings, for garnish

Instructions

- Preheat the oven to 350 degrees F and spray the pie dish with cooking spray
- For making the crust; take a food processor and pulse the graham crackers in it till you get a fine form
- Now move this to a medium bowl and add sugar along with melted butter and salt and mix well to combine properly
- Now press the graham cracker mixture to the pie dish and bake it till the crust turns golden. This should take approx 10 minutes
- Let it cool down to room temperature
- Now for making the pie, take a medium-sized bowl and whisk both milk and egg yolk till it has combined thoroughly
- Take a small saucepan and add sugar along with cayenne, cinnamon, salt, cornstarch and whisk it well
- Now add the milk-egg mixture and whisk again to make sure there are no lumps whatsoever
- Bring the whole mix to boil and then reduce the heat and allow it to simmer for a minute
- Remove from the heat source and stir again in butter and add vanilla and chocolate chips till you find that everything has thoroughly melted
- Now pour this mixture to the prepared crust and let it refrigerate for a couple of hours. It should get firm by then
- Now take the marshmallow creme and fold them into the whipped topping and spread on the very center of the pie

- Top it with chocolate shavings
- Serve

Tres Leches Cake

When in Mexico, there is no way you can miss out on this iconic tres leches cake. This butter cake that is soaked in three different kinds of milk will melt in your mouth and teleport you directly to the heavens.

Ingredients

- 3 large eggs
- 1 package butter recipe golden cake mix
- 1/2 cup of softened butter
- 2/3 cup; 2% milk
- 1 tsp of vanilla extract

Topping:

- 1 can of sweetened condensed milk; 14 ounces
- 1 can of evaporated milk; 12 ounces
- 1 cup of heavy whipping cream

Whipped cream:

- 3 tbsp of confectioners' sugar
- 1 cup of heavy whipping cream
- 1 tsp of vanilla extract

Instructions

- Preheat the oven to 350 degrees F
- Grease a baking pan thoroughly to be used later
- Now take a large bowl and add the cake mix along with softened butter, vanilla milk, and eggs. Beat it on low speed for half a minute
- Now beat it on medium speed for a couple of minutes and then move it to the pan
- Bake for half an hour
- Now cool on a wire rack for approximately 15 minutes
- Take a measuring cup and whisk the topping ingredients in it until they have completely blended
- Now poke holes on the top of the warm cake
- Pour the milk mixture over the cake slowly to fill the holes
- Cool for half an hour
- Refrigerate the cake by covering it overnight
- Now take a bowl and beat the cream till it thickens
- Add the confectioners' sugar along with vanilla and beat it till you get a soft peak
- Spread this all over the cake
- Serve

Flan Borracho

This is yet another delicacy that enjoys tremendous popularity all over Mexico. This is a great dish which will make you crave for more and then some more. The fact that it isn't hard to make further adds to its growing popularity.

Ingredients

- 6 eggs
- 1 can of condensed milk; sweetened; 12 oz
- 1 ½ tsp of vanilla
- ¾ cup of sugar
- 1 ½ cups of whole milk
- 2 tbsp of dark rum
- 1/8 tsp of salt

Instructions

- Keep the oven rack in the lower part of your oven and then preheat it to 325 degrees F
- Now melt the sugar on low heat and make sure to stir often. This will help you make the caramel sauce.
- Pour the melted sugar/caramel sauce to a baking pan and spread it quickly before it starts to harden. Make sure to coat the bottom of the pan evenly with this melted sugar mix
- Take a new bowl and mix all the ingredients in it till you get a smooth consistency
- Now pour this mix on the pan over the top of the caramel syrup
- Set a water bath by placing the flan in the larger baking pan of the warm water. The water should come halfway up the flan dish
- Now bake it for an hour
- Take it out of the oven and let it cool
- When it has cooled, refrigerate it for an hour
- Now cover the flan pan with a flat dish and let it rest
- Separate the flan from the dish and flip it
- Serve

No Fry Fried Ice Cream

Love ice cream but don't like to have things greasy and messy? Well, this is the recipe you have been looking for! We will wrap up the dessert section with this ultimate bonus ice cream recipe, after all, it is the end which makes the tale so sweet, isn't it!

Ingredients

- 6 cups of crushed Wheaties cereal
- 1 gallon of softened vanilla ice cream
- 5 tbsp of corn syrup
- 2 tbsp of white sugar
- 2 tsp of ground cinnamon
- 3 tbsp of melted butter
- Whipped topping, caramel syrup, chocolate syrup, and cinnamon

Instructions

- Take a small bowl and combine crushed cereal along with corn syrup, sugar, cinnamon, and butter. Mix well and set aside.
- Shape the ice-cream into equal-sized balls measuring 3 inches and roll it in the cereal mixture
- Press lightly to make sure that the ball is well coated
- Place the ice cream balls in muffin tins and then freeze it until it is ready to serve
- Serve with syrup and whipped topping and add a sprinkle of cinnamon

Conclusion

So now that we have come to the end of the book, we are pretty sure that you must be pumped up about cooking the different meals. There are tons of recipes that we shared and the fact that they were all segregated means that you have the option of perusing the section you deem most appropriate and then you can go ahead and carry out with your cooking.

The underlying idea behind this book was to mainly help you understand the key constituents that make Mexican food so special.

As we all know, Mexican food is all about getting the ingredients right. Until and unless the spices are all in tandem and the perfect food is present in the right mix, it shouldn't be easy to get the taste right. So, you should keep an eye out on the specifics of how to follow and adhere to the cooking instructions and then follow them to make lip-smacking recipes.

We all believe that every meal made with all your heart is sure to ring in the right flavors. Regardless of where in the world do you live, there are very few people who aren't hooked to the authentic taste of rich Mexican cuisine. With this book, we are sure you will be able to satiate your food buds and savor the rich delicacies and the perfect taste of too many varying recipes.

From tacos to pizza, pasta, sauces, dips, and even soups; this book is replete with the right set of information which is bound to make a key difference. If you love food or even if you are hooked to cooking, this book is the perfect pick for you. It is bound to fill you with a sense of sheer joy and pleasure and while making these dishes, you will surely be able to enjoy the whole art of it.

So, go through the book as many times as needed and make sure to follow the details. Ideally, we would like you to do a mix and match of the different recipes in here so that your food buds will have ample variety to look forward to. Trust us, the recipes are all tried and tested and the food is going to be so good that you are going to fall for it.

Make sure to let us know as to how useful you found this book to be and if you have been addicted to Mexican cuisine as well. Never forget the need to use the best of sauces and dips because it is these extras that infuse the perfect and typical Mexican flavor in every dish!

So, enjoy your meal and give your cooking experience an all-new high that both you and the people you cook for are going to absolutely love!